Treating Abused Adolescents

Darlene Anderson Merchant

with the assistance of the
Adolescent Victim Counseling Program
Storefront/Youth Action
Richfield, MN

and

Steve Lepsinski
Mike Wolff
Carol Wickers-Schulman
Merle Green

LP **Learning Publications, Inc.**
MONTREAL   HOLMES BEACH, FL

ISBN 1-55691-017-7

Learning Publications, Inc.
5351 Gulf Drive
P.O. Box 1338
Holmes Beach, FL 34218-1338

Library of Congress Catalogue Card Nunmber 89-084977

Printing: 6 5 4 3   Year: 10 9 8 7 6

Printed in the United States of America.

TABLE OF CONTENTS

1920

105291

ACKNOWLEDGEMENTS

Treating Abused Adolescents has been a project of the Adolescent Victim Counseling Program at Storefront/Youth Action, Richfield, MN. It was and prepared under the direction of Steve Lepinski, M.H.A., Executive Director; Mike Wolff, Program Director; and the Board of Directors. An initial draft of *Chapters* 2 and 5 was written by Carol Wickers-Schulman. Additions and revisions were written by Darlene Anderson Merchant. Merle Green was our Editor.

I wish to acknowledge the work performed by the staff at Storefront/Youth Action that has provided the basis for this manual. I worked with James Badiner, Kathleen Conlon, Jane Geppert, Barbara Mohr, Joan Weber, and others to develop and carry out the program. Chris Servaty from the Sexual Violence Center co-led victim groups at Storefront/Youth Action and contributed to the growth of the program. Mike Wolff, Debra Magnuson and Dr. Patrick Carnes should be recognized for developing the program in 1979. In addition, a thank you to our support staff, Kathy Anderson, Ann Welna and Anne Benson.

I also wish to thank our clients who, through therapy, have let us know what is important in helping them to grow and change. Case names used in this work are fictitious, and some histories are actually based on composites, to provide better illustrations.

Partial funding for the project was provided by the Minnesota Juvenile Justice Advisory Committee.

DAM

1

Introduction

In recent years, the reporting of adolescent abuse has increased together with the need for therapy for victims and their families. But professionals who must identify and treat abuse still have few resources from which to draw. That is why this program guide was written: to help therapists who work with abused adolescents and their families. It takes professional therapists from the identification stages through the process of long-term therapy.

The techniques and suggestions offered reflect our experiences as therapists in a counseling agency for adolescents, with a special program for abused adolescents and their families. Our program is based on the belief that family therapy should, if possible, be an important part of treatment in most abuse cases. That is because families in which abuse occurs are significantly dysfunctional. But even children who are abused by outsiders, sometimes feel emotionally neglected in their families and thus vulnerable to abuse outside of the home. Others simply need the support of a caring family.

However, the program suggested here also helps abused adolescents whose families will not become involved or are unavailable. Young people can often make significant progress in therapy on their own or with surrogate families.

This program is concerned with all kinds of abuse to children and adolescents—emotional, physical, and neglect, as well as sexual abuse. However, the treatment needs of sexually abused adolescents, ages 12-18, are of the most concern in this discussion. The terms "children" and "adolescents" are used when it is important to differentiate between them, such as when adolescents were abused when they were young and the early abuse is still causing problems.

Professionals are increasingly aware of the problem of adolescents who are being abused. The news media is reporting it more regularly and it is the subject of network movies and documentaries. There have also been court cases involving child abuse which have been widely publicized. The 1983 study by the American Humane Association estimates that 1.5 million children are abused or neglected annually. Of this, 29% involve adolescent abuse or neglect. These figures are based on all cases reported to government agencies. They represent a 121% increase since 1976. Clearly, there is a great deal of adolescent abuse.

These and other abuse statistics are probably low. The families are usually secretive and distrustful of outsiders. Children are often threatened with beatings or exclusion from the family if they report abuse. Professionals sometimes lack adequate identification skills to know when and how to ask about possible abuse. Some workers avoid the topics or choose not to report abuse out of fear that it will affect the therapeutic relationship or endanger the child.

People are less likely to report adolescent maltreatment than child maltreatment for several reasons. They believe that the misbehavior of adolescents' invites abuse or that adolescents can run away if it occurs.

As shown in Table 1, the largest category of reported abuse to adolescents is sexual abuse. Sixty percent of those who were sexually abused were young women.

Table 1
Adolescent Maltreatment*

Sexual Maltreatment	40.6% of reported cases
Emotional Maltreatment	31.9%
Minor or Unspecified Physical Injury	30.0%
Multiple Maltreatment	27.0%
Other Maltreatment	26.2%
Major Physical Injury	15.9%
Deprivation of Necessities	18.2%

---

*Source: American Humane Association

Unfortunately, the sexual abuse to adolescent males is not sufficiently recognized by many professionals. They tend to believe that males are the offenders and that girls are mostly the victims. They also believe that boys are better able to protect themselves than girls in the event they are sexually assaulted. Consequently, fewer adolescent males than females are identified as victims of sexual abuse.

THEIR OFFENDERS

In most cases of adolescent sexual abuse, apart from acquaintance rape, the adult offender is a parent or parent surrogate. Although offenders tend to be male and their victims female, this is not always the case.

Men are most responsible for the sexual abuse of boys. Although most literature only discusses sexual abuse of girls by males (fathers, step-fathers, uncles) it is our and others experience that sexual abuse by mothers and stepmothers also occurs. Sibling incest is also being identified more frequently.

2

Identifying Abuse

As helping professionals, we must be able to identify adolescents who show signs of emotional, physical, and sexual abuse. Many adolescents show explicit signs of abuse, while some show signs indirectly because of other problems in their lives. We need to look at every case individually.

While each abuse has distinct symptoms, these are some underlying characteristics and issues common to most abuse victims. Abuse victims often:

- dislike themselves;
- experience feelings of shame;
- feel worthless and hopeless, believe they are no good;
- do not trust others, especially their parents and other adults;
- feel that they caused the abuse;
- feel angry and depressed.

Typically, abused adolescents respond by feeling depressed, exhibiting low self-esteem and entering into unhealthy relationships or by feeling angry and acting in aggressive ways.

DEPRESSION, LOW SELF-ESTEEM AND UNHEALTHY RELATIONSHIPS

Abused adolescents often feel depressed, have low self-esteem and withdraw from others.

Abused adolescents may show signs of **depression** by:

- mutilating themselves;

- expressing suicidal ideation or making suicide attempts;

- having trouble sleeping;

- changing eating habits, gaining or losing weight;

- showing signs of hopelessness and helplessness; and

- being listless and showing little energy.

They may show signs of **low self-esteem** and shame by:

- indicating that they are not likeable;

- withdrawing from others;

- using negative body language, such as downcast, head and eyes and slumping body.

Abused adolescents often enter into **unhealthy relationships** by:

- accepting the exploitation by others;

- believing that they are unworthy of friends;

- staying in destructive relationships;

- placing themselves in unprotected dangerous situations;

- acting helpless, and non-assertive and vulnerable; and

- being especially gullible when someone suggests that they are lovable.

Case Example. Joan came to our agency after being raped when she and her cousin took a ride with two strange men. Joan told her cousin that she did not want to get into the car. However, when her cousin said she'd leave her there alone, she consented.

Joan was emotionally abused by her parents, who told her that she was not intelligent like her brother or pretty like her sister. She was 30 pounds overweight, but her mother undermined her attempts to diet, by giving her fattening food. Joan dressed carelessly, had very few friends, and kept to herself at school and at home. She lacked assertiveness and had a desperate need for attention. She had been abused by boys in the past.

Joan started therapy with an interview at which only her mother was present (no other family members would come). At the intake, Joan's mother was very verbal and controlling. Joan, however, was very quiet, had very little energy, and did not speak up or look disturbed when her mother said things with which Joan disagreed. Joan denied any suicidal thoughts or attempts. She said that she slept a great deal—up to 12 hours a night. Joan said she gained 5 pounds since being raped.

Joan attended individual counseling and developed a trusting relationship with her therapist. After about six sessions, she was able to initiate some conversations, maintain some eye contact, show interest in her group work and stated what she would like to gain from therapy. When Joan began group therapy, she would sit on a pillow in the corner and she responded only when questions were addressed to her. She kept her eyes and head down during most of the group meetings and did not chat with the other members at break time.

Early on, Joan showed signs of depression: weight gain, little energy, passiveness, a helpless demeanor and excessive sleeping. In the beginning, she also showed signs of low self-esteem and had difficulty initiating conversations at the beginning of both individual and group therapy. In the early months of therapy, she avoided casual conversations with the other group members. She physically isolated herself in group by sitting in the corner with her head down.

Joan also allowed herself to be manipulated in relationships with others. She chose to walk with her cousin in an isolated area without voicing her opinion. She also went along with her cousin in accepting a ride with a stranger even though she didn't want to. She was prepared to endanger her own safety so as not to risk alienating her cousin. (This does not mean that either Joan or her cousin were responsible for the rape since the responsibility for the rape lies with the offender.) Joan has allowed herself to be used sexually by boys in the past because she saw herself as unlikable. She found it very difficult to open up first to the therapist and then to group members.

As she worked on her goals in group, she opened up more. After a year, she was a "senior member," telling new members how group operated, taking time for herself and her issues, and supporting other members. She had made friends in group that she now saw socially. She was ready to leave the group.

AGGRESSION

Aggressive adolescents who "act out" are well known to helping professionals because they behave in such obviously inappropriate ways. They express their feelings of anger, distrust, and hopelessness with people and institutions; and there seems to be a high need for recognition and attention through anti-social behavior.

Incest victims have had so little success in resisting their abusers that they often hide their feelings until they find an outlet such as arson, vandalism, theft, prostitution, or abusing others sexually.

Adolescents who have experienced sexual abuse may:

- be angry at everyone or at groups of people such as males, females or adults;

- act extremely self-centered;

- seem not to care about anyone else;

- act tough;

- refuse to get close to anyone;

- start fights; and

- show off a lot.

Adolescents often pick fights soon after being abused. They may also "push buttons," knowing exactly what will irritate, embarrass, or hurt people the most. These anti-social acts are ways of attracting attention, connecting with others, expressing anger, defending against pain, and keeping people at a distance so as not to be hurt.

Case Example. Susan is a 13 year old client who was neglected and abused emotionally and physically by her mother and stepfather. She was also sexually abused by an older neighbor boy. She and her siblings are now living in an adoptive home after she was removed from her mother's custody. Susan has many problems including abandonment, a shameful feeling that she is unlovable and a distrust of adults and boys. She has had much difficulty with relationships in the past: she sexually molested a boy while babysitting; she cut a student's pants at school and convinced the class that someone else was responsible; she lied a great deal and she regularly got into fights with her adoptive mother.

In therapy, Susan found it difficult to recognize her feelings. She tried to avoid relating any of her pain and anger to her past. She would "recite" answers to assignments rather than let herself feel the reality of the past. When she joined group therapy, she was self-centered, demanding time for herself, but being inattentive to others. She sometimes disrupted the group to say how much she disliked the others and fought with the group leaders. She was hurtful to a classmate. Underneath her aggressiveness and self-centeredness, she felt insecure and afraid to open up. These negative behaviors indicate that Susan had feelings with which she was not dealing. Now Susan is able to be more open about her feelings and act in positive ways toward others.

Signs Common to Both Types. Although some sexually abused adolescents may withdraw or act out aggressively, it is not uncommon for them to show signs in other unhealthy ways. For example, tough-acting adolescents who let down their guard may show signs of depression and withdrawal. Adolescents who are passive at school may act out at home, perhaps by physically or sexually abusing their siblings. Sexually abused adolescents may well become abusive with other people. They know abuse as a common family pattern even though they suffer emotionally from its effects. Techniques for managing these abusive tendencies will be discussed later.

Being abused also tends to affect one's school work. Many abused adolescents do badly in school and have poor attendance records. They often cannot concentrate in school because they are so preoccupied with their past or expected abuse. Other victims want to be in school and become perfect students in order to disassociate themselves from their families. Some children have had to fight their parents in order to be allowed to attend school.

Many abused adolescents refuse to take responsibility for their actions. They may lie or steal, get caught, and still deny that they are responsible. They worry more about their own punishment than about others who suffer because of what they have done. If abused adolescents are not consistently rewarded for socially acceptable behavior, they may have little reason to act correctly. They develop such attitudes as "I have to take what I can get because no one else will look out for me," and "adults aren't honest—so why should I be?"

Some abused adolescents run away, risking further sexual abuse or they turn to prostitution for survival. Others use alcohol or other illicit drugs to escape their turbulent feelings and then they become chemically dependent.

It is not unusual for adolescents who have been abused to distrust adults who remind them of their offenders. When their therapists are the same sex as their offenders, they may find it difficult to develop a trusting relationship. Similarly, abused adolescents may have problems with any of their teachers who remind them of their abusers. They may get in trouble in class, undermine their teacher's authority, rally support against her, and withdraw.

Many female and some male victims of abuse develop eating disorders, including anorexia nervosa, bulimia, and compulsive overeating. These adolescents may use food to distance themselves from their feelings, harm or reward themselves, or alleviate tensions.

Anorexics, who starve themselves, use food to take control over one part of their lives, since everything else seems to be out of control. Although they appear passive and frail, they are actively self-destructive and often express anger manipulatively and dishonestly. Their refusal to eat is a nonverbal statement about not wanting to grow up. It may be a way to avoid being sexual or functional in a chaotic environment. A part of them wants to disappear.

Bulimics, who eat excessively and then purge, turn to food when under stress. They see themselves alternatively as bad and good. As "bad" persons, they are filled with shame and they find it difficult to share hurtful parts of their past. As "good" persons, they play idealized roles such as the "cheer-leader," or other roles in school, all the while hiding their secret feelings.

Compulsive overeaters sometimes use food as a "friend" to help them feel loved, cared for, emotionally nourished, and complete. They often dissociate themselves from their bodies. Physically and sexually abused adolescents may want to forget about their bodies being abused and "disown" themselves at the moment abuse is taking place. By overeating, victims may seek to distance themselves from others, thus avoiding sexual or intimate encounters——something a sexually abused adolescent often fears.

EMOTIONAL ABUSE

Adolescents who have been severely abused, are likely to show signs of low self-esteem through withdrawal behaviors. Typically, they try to please other people who frequently take advantage of them. In addition, they may be ill continually and complain of medical problems. The symptoms are often stress-related and used as a way to get attention and affection. School nurses sometimes uncover abuse among students who regularly report being sick.

PHYSICAL ABUSE

Adolescents who have been physically abused will most often act out. They may act overly tough or be very withdrawn until they start a fight for some simple thing, such as being touched. On the other hand, they may react with oversubmissiveness. They may look to those who abuse them for permission to talk. They are motivated by fear.

Some young adolescents (ages 12-14) who have been physically abused express anger by initially hitting and shoving each other in a joking way. Then, their anger comes out in serious fights. Young abused victims may not know how to be intimate in appropriate ways.

SEXUAL ABUSE

Adolescents who have been sexually abused are likely to exhibit either withdrawal or acting out behaviors. If their abuse involves another family member, the adolescent probably has a care-taking role within the family. Often the child is forced into a spouse relationship with an offender. Along with sexual obligations come responsibilities for caring for siblings, doing housework (especially for female victims), and bringing in money (especially for male victims). These children sense that they have a different relationship with their parents than do their siblings. They may believe that their importance, and perhaps only value, derives from taking care of others and being sexual. They often take on the same role in other relationships by serving people without taking into account their own needs.

Some sexually abused adolescents have extreme difficulty in friendships with others who are of the same sex. They may:

- feel inadequate and unworthy of respect;

- show disrespect for persons of their sex;

- have learned that persons of their sex are worthless;

- feel threatened by persons of the same sex.

For some adolescents in abusive relationships, sex becomes the major focus of their lives. This becomes apparent in several ways, depending on the individual:

- promiscuous behavior;

- constantly using sexual innuendos;

- being extremely flirtatious with adults as well as their peers, dressing seductively;

- being overly concerned about possibly being homosexual;

- talking disparagingly about homosexuals;

- exhibiting generalized anger and distrust of people of the opposite sex;

- gravitating toward those of the opposite sex;

- sexually abusive to others. They think that sex will meet their needs for intimacy, personal importance and power. Thus, as was done to them, they force others to submit to abuse. Some adolescents are sexually abusive out of a desperate need to prove that they are not homosexual.

On the opposite end of the spectrum, there are abused adolescents who shun sexuality altogether.

They usually try to:

- avoid physical or social contact with anyone of the same sex as their offender;

- make themselves as unattractive as possible and wear clothes that hide their bodies. Sexually abused young women may assume masculine, athletic appearances that they think will be unattractive to males.

3

Family Dynamics

Family system therapy treats the family as an entity whose parts are intimately connected. Each family member affects the others. Yet, the family unit itself is separate from and greater than any of the individual members. It is an institution with patterns and beliefs that are often transferred from one generation to the next. So, when we look at abusive families, we must explore both the characteristics of their members and the interactions that go on within these families.

MULTI-GENERATIONAL ABUSE

It is very common that abusive parents were abused or neglected when they were children. However, the abuse that parents received as children may not be the same as that which they now engage in. However, there are characteristics that they pass on. Victimizers tend to have low self-esteem, feel insecure, and have many unmet dependency needs. They imitate the behaviors learned when they were growing up. One typical learned behavior is to react to stress by becoming abusive.

Case Example. Jackie and her family were referred to our agency by the court because of incest. At the time of referral, Jackie was 16 years old, a good student, and an overly responsible family member. She had three younger sisters whom she cared for when her mother was at work and at night school. Jackie's grandfather began to sexually abuse her when she was eight years old. The abuse by the grandfather occurred monthly when the family visited him.

It stopped when Jackie was twelve. Shortly afterwards, Jackie's father began to fondle her. Within several months he began fellatio which eventually led to penetration. This continued for about three years. Then he started victimizing the next oldest daughter, Linda. After several months of abuse, Linda reported it to her mother who said, "If it happens again, let me know." Linda finally told a school counselor who reported it to child protection services. Her father was charged with criminal sexual conduct and ordered by the court to seek treatment.

What is significant about this family and typical of so many others is multiple victimization; neither Jackie's father or grandfather was aware of the other's abuse; neither Jackie nor Linda were aware of the other's victimization. The course of therapy in this case is described in the next chapter.

ENMESHMENT-DISENGAGEMENT PATTERNS

One way of looking at relationships within abusive families is to measure the extent to which members are enmeshed with or disengaged from each other's lives. In families where abuse occurs the children are usually not allowed to be different from their parents, or to feel unique. The parents expect their spouse and children to meet all of their needs for affection, belonging, financial security, and self-esteem. Since no one can fulfill all of these needs, the parents and children are left feeling dissatisfied and incomplete. They want someone on whom they can be dependent. They feel that by themselves, they are incomplete or missing in abilities to satisfy themselves or others. Since they feel incomplete by themselves, they often put up with abuse to keep the complete family together.

In disengaged families, the members feel lonely and isolated. The children often feel rejected and unwanted, and, in fact, child neglect is not uncommon. Members often leave because they do not feel the support of the family unit. Children may marry early, get in trouble, and be sent away or they may find other escape routes out of the home. Parents from families who separate may not stay in contact with their children. On the other hand, parents in such families who remain at home may come and go to suit their own desires rather than the needs of their children.

Adolescents from disengaged families may try to fill security and family needs by clinging to unhealthy or destructive friendships outside of the home. Or they may try to find adults outside the home to nurture them. Sometimes they form positive relationships, sometimes harmful ones.

SHAME PATTERNS

Shaming is the process of degrading people by denying their self-worth. Like other abuse, it is often introduced into families by adults who were shamed as children. As parents, they often set expectations that are unattainable for their children or cannot be met. When their children don't know what is expected of them or cannot meet their expectations, they are often labeled as "no good," "You'll never amount to anything," or "You can't do anything right." These parents seldom give their children opportunities to make amends or prove themselves. Also, they are not usually given clear messages about what is expected of them or when they must accomplish their expectations.

Children who have been shamed want to be accepted by their parents very much. They try and try (usually unsuccessfully) to get their attention, caring, and approval. Defeated, they try to meet their own needs alone; or they may rely on others to meet them indirectly. Yet they still feel insecure, unwanted and afraid of abandonment. They tend to cover up these feelings and relate to others by playing roles such as clown, seducer, liar, or pleaser.

Case Example. Sean is a 12 year old boy who came for counseling with his foster family. In his foster home, Sean often lied, stole, and avoided his foster parents. Sean had been neglected by his natural parents. His parents were separated, and his mother worked nights, slept days, and went out with friends in the evening. Sean was expected to make meals for his younger siblings and keep household appliances working and the wood pile stocked. When he was unable to carry out these responsibilities, he was berated. He was also belittled for not being more active in sports or spending more time with friends, even though it was impossible for him to participate in these activities.

Sean was given too many responsibilities for a boy of his age and he received neither direction for carrying out his tasks nor credit for what he did accomplish. In addition, his mother did not take Sean's needs into account. As a result of these circumstances, Sean learned not to trust or turn to adults for guidance. He found it hard to be open about his feelings with his foster parents and other adults. Sean's attitudes are typical of shamed children.

Parents who threaten punishment which they do not carry out set up a no-win situation. When parents later acknowledge that the punishment they have threatened is unjustified or allow their children to talk them out of it, they undermine their own authority. They reinforce manipulation as a constructive way of relating to others. Furthermore, they deprive their children of clearly set rules upon which to rely.

If children internalize the shame they experience in their families, they sustain feelings of inadequacy even in the absence of outside criticism. When they look at their accomplishments and find imperfections, they take this as proof that they are worthless individuals. They become overly sensitive and they interpret ordinary comments as personal denigration.

People who have been abused usually feel both shame and rage. They are usually embarrassed and secretive about their being abused. They often feel bad, unclean and that they are to blame for the abuse. Feelings of rage result from excessive anger at perpetrators. These feelings of rage and shame are likely to continue into adulthood and then increase the likelihood of abusing others. People who feel ashamed sometimes act out their rage by becoming abusive to others. Then feeling even more shame and the anger toward themselves, they further abuse others. The cycle of abuse continues on and on.

THE IMPORTANCE OF POWER

In abusive families, parents and their children tend to take on either overly powerful or powerless roles. Usually there is one dominant adult who is abusive to one or more of the others. Of course, an abusive adult always has more power than the children in the family. This is why victims of child abuse often feel powerless to help themselves. A number of points can be made about the role of power in the home.

- All parents—loved or not—exercise emotional power over their young children. They are usually larger, stronger, and more worldly. They provide a place to stay. (Whether or not that place is safe is secondary.) Many abusive parents use threats to force children to comply with their demands and to prevent them from telling outsiders about being abused.

- Children in abusive families are taught by the parents to believe that physical, emotional or sexual abuse is "normal" and that they as children are to blame for being abused.

- The family is very important to all children. Abused children, in particular, are afraid to lose what security they have by leaving home, talking back or disobeying. (They are led to believe that their parents have all the power, that they can throw them out of the house). Abused children are also likely to be afraid they may not be able to survive outside of their homes.

- Many abused adolescents fear for the safety and care of their younger siblings or of a non-abusive parent if they were to leave home.

- Even after abused adolescents leave home, they often continue to feel powerless. To make matters worse, many of those who are "on the run" are so emotionally vulnerable that they put themselves in situations where they are victimized again by other adults or their peers.

In order to assert their own power or release hurt and angry feelings, abused adolescents often: rebel against their parents, act out in their community, misuse food, alcohol, and drugs, or worse, take their own lives.

Case Example.   Joe is an eleven year old boy who was referred to us by the school for skipping classes and having a poor attitude.   In the course of counseling, it was discovered that Joe had been physically and emotionally abused by his parents for the past three years.   Joe's mother had been battered since her marriage twelve years ago.   Joe's father was an alcoholic who used hard drugs and alcohol over twelve years but was never treated for his addiction.   When Joe's father was drinking, he would come home and beat Joe's mother.   If Joe tried to intervene to protect his mother, his father would hit him, push him against the wall, grasp his arm until it was bruised, slap his face and pull his hair.   This kind of abuse would happen about once a week.   At other times, Joe's father would blame him for the tension and fighting in their home. He would also ask Joe if his mother was seeing other men.   If Joe said yes, his father would beat his mother.   If he said no, his father would beat him for lying.

It is clear that the father of Joe subjugated his wife and son into powerless roles.   Joe would try to defend his mother and feared for both his and his mother's safety.   Because Joe had no way of venting his anger, and because he felt powerless with his father, he expressed his frustration indirectly: he acted out at school and he related poorly with his peers.

ROLE REVERSALS AND THE ABSENCE OF BOUNDARIES

Abusive families, especially those involved in sexual abuse, have difficulty setting healthy limits to what is tolerated.   In non-abusive families, for example, there are boundaries between parents and their children. The parents have an intimacy with one another that is private and they are not sexual with their children. The parents in a non-abusive home guide and discipline their children.

On the other hand, in abusive homes, the boundaries are less clear. One child in an abusive family may be given more and more parental responsibilities, such as caring for his brothers and sisters, maintaining the house, or making money to cover the family's expenses. This may occur because one parent is absent or out working when the children are home. Adolescents in abusive families often feel total responsibility for their siblings, refer to them as the "kids" (even though they are very close in age). They may even regard their brothers and sisters as their own children.

Another example of role reversal is when parents confide in their children as they normally would to a spouse. When such is the case, sexual abuse may also occur. Children who are promoted to the spouse role usually draw both positive and negative experiences from such a relationship. They may:

- receive compliments on their good looks, sexiness or ability to manage the household;

- feel proud and special that they are able to meet their parent's needs where their other parent is unable or unwilling;

- receive gifts that other family members don't; and

- enjoy for a time, their relationships with their parent.

Childhood victims:

- have difficulty recognizing when they are being abused when they receive short term rewards; and

- they thereby feel guilty when they do recognize the abuse. They think having taken rewards makes them guilty.

Victims of role reversal must cope with many negative experiences. One of the worst is the invasion of their personal boundary:

- "spouse" children must provide sexual activity or face frightening consequences (Their parent may threaten them with harm, abandonment, or exile); and

- children placed in adult roles are not allowed to enjoy childhood. Often, there may be no privacy in bathrooms, bedrooms may not have doors and personal property may not be respected.

Role reversal can take the opposite form, too, wherein abused parents who enter marriage or relationships with low self-esteem tend to take on their child's role. Thereby, abusive parents tend to demand that their children give priority to parental needs over their own needs as children.

Case Example. Jackie and her family were referred to us by the court because of incest. She was sixteen years old, a good student, and an overly responsible family member who had been sexually abused by both her father and grandfather. Jackie's father had strong feelings of inadequacy, particularly as his wife (Jackie's mother) became more distant. The family had almost no contact with other families or involvement in community activities. There were role reversals and blurred role boundaries: Jackie's father felt powerless and child-like; her mother abdicated parental and marital responsibilities to Jackie; her father was more emotionally and sexually involved with Jackie than with his wife; and the spouses had trouble maintaining an intimate relationship.

ARRESTED DEVELOPMENT

Abused adolescents often do not develop at the same rate as other young people. Those who were abused as children may have speech problems, or find it difficult to develop friendships outside the family. Even though they may be old beyond their years in terms of sexual experience or household responsibilities, they may appear much younger than their biological age in other areas.

PARENTING

Abusive parents are usually unable to identify and adequately express their feelings. Rather than talk directly with others about their concerns and then find ways to resolve their problems, they tend to deny their feelings and/or release them in some of the following ways:

- The emotional abuser tends to express anger and pain by belittling other people.

- A parent may feel overwhelmed at work and reacts by not providing adequate care to his child.

- The physical abuser often lets pain, shame, anger, and frustration build up until he or she "explodes" with a physical attack.

- The sexual abuser acts out his feelings with inappropraite sexual behavior.

For many abusive parents, there is no direct causal relationship between their children's behavior and the abuse that they impose. Often, children are abused for innocent behavior because their parents are upset about something else.

As a result, abused children have little sense of how to avoid being abused and what is socially appropriate behavior. This creates considerable tension in their lives.

Case Example. John talked about how his father kicked him once when he was upset about problems at his office. John was doing nothing out of the ordinary, simply talking on the phone, which at any other time, would have been accepted.

Some abusive parents who demand rigid compliance with their expectations and yet give their children very little freedom to learn to meet these expectations, inflict extreme punishments for failing.

LIFE CHANGES

Life changes and stresses can cause abuse to occur and reoccur. Sometimes emotional or physical abuse occurs only at ages 2-3 and again in adolescence. During adolescence, young people struggle to develop their own identities and, at the same time, maintain a secure place within their families. When they begin to test their limits and their parent's control, families feel pressure.

Adolescents may contest their parents issues more readily than younger children because they want to be autonomous from their parents. They have differing opinions, and they may desire more freedom to socialize with their peers. These parents may react by imposing rigid restrictions. When parents cannot control their adolescents' behavior, they may react abusively.

While adolescents are struggling with separation issues, their parents may be struggling with their own mid-life crises. The parents may wonder about the ways they have chosen to live their lives and the values they hold. This time is not the most opportune one for coping with a teenager's identity crisis. And of course, other stressors that increase the likelihood of abuse in the home include unemployment, marital problems, divorce and illness.

4

Beginning Family Therapy

In the case of a perpetrator and a victim who are members of the same family, therapy is often difficult to initiate and sustain. <u>When abuse is uncovered, all family members react with fear, anger and denial.</u>

Families who have been isolated and secretive find themselves suddenly questioned by outsiders. Offenders and others may fear prosecution or the break-up of their families. The spouse who is dependent on the offender may be frightened at the prospect of surviving on his or her own. This is also true of the children.

Many parents and siblings of abused children get angry at the victim of abuse for possibly causing the family to break up. They may even accuse the victim of telling family secrets or telling lies. Sometimes family members get angry at outsiders for intruding and threatening the existence of the family. At other times, they feel relief that others know and will help them.

In sexual abuse cases, offenders, spouses, and siblings often deny that any abuse has occurred. Spouses risk destroying the illusion that their families are perfect when they believe that a partner has had sex with their child. They must acknowledge that their partners have betrayed them. They are thereby forced to reexamine their beliefs about marriage and consider their own possible role in the abuse.

Unabused siblings are forced to look at the abusing parents in a different light. Offending parents will often deny their abusiveness. In sexual abuse cases, they often minimize their fault and blame their victims, in order to avoid feeling shame and failure. In cases of emotional and physical abuse or neglect, the parents may deny their children's allegations, asserting that they have the right to discipline their children as they wish, or that what they did was not abusive. In many cases, abusive parents resist counseling because they are afraid of seeing themselves as imperfect parents.

ENTERING THERAPY

For all the above reasons, families where abuse has occurred often resist coming to therapy. The more severe the abuse and the enmeshment of the family, the more they resist counseling. Rarely do they seek help on their own initiative. Many undergo treatment only if ordered by a court.

Offenders may be charged through criminal court and be ordered by the court to receive therapy. They may be threatened with severe consequences if they don't follow through. These threats may vary depending on the crime, the judge, the individuals bringing charges, and the investigating officers.

Referrals to therapy often come from juvenile courts. If the victim is also charged with an offense that may be related to their victimization, the judge or jury may order therapy for the adolescent alone or for the family. However, juvenile court cannot force parents to get therapy. On the other hand, they can threaten the removal of custody of the child from the parents. As a result, abusive parents often accept family therapy because they want to retain custody of their children.

Court orders are sometimes helpful because they force families into therapy who would not otherwise face their responsibility. As their problems become more difficult to face, they may continue to come to therapy only because of the threats imposed by the court. Eventually, if the therapy is successful, they will make personal commitments to work toward healthier behaviors.

Sometimes adolescents who want help for themselves will be referred to you. In such a case, parent may refuse therapy but allow their children to attend. Older adolescents will work toward separating their feelings and beliefs from those of their families. Eventually, they may be able to communicate their feelings and tell their parents what they need from them. Then their families may become involved because they have observed the positive effects of therapy.

We often ask families to come for treatment on the pretext of "helping their child" or "letting them know how their child is trying to change." Sometimes parents will have their first experience with counseling during these sessions and later identify their own desire for change.

A young person sometimes charges his or her parent with abuse. If resultant prosecution is successful, the court may order family therapy. Therapists can encourage families to become involved by responding to the feelings of each member and offering assistance and hope. They can also stress how important it is to stop their abuse before their children are hurt more and they develop into abusive parents themselves.

UNCOVERING ABUSE

If a family is already involved in therapy and child abuse has not yet been disclosed, the following may increase the possibility that they will remain in treatment after the abuse is disclosed:

1. Tell everyone in the family during the first session, before any abusive disclosure occurs, that you are legally required to report child abuse.

2. Once abuse has been disclosed, tell them as much as you can about what happens when abuse is reported, without being speculative or inaccurate. Encourage those who consider themselves to be child abusers to call and report the abuse themselves to the proper authorities. You still must make a formal report.

3. Let the victims who talk about their abuse know that you believe them.

4. Let the parents know that you believe that they are doing the best they can at this time, while being firm about stopping their abusiveness.

   - Tell them that you have worked with offenders before (if this is true), that you know that offenders are struggling and hurting, and that help is available for them.

   - Help the parents to talk about their struggles. You may ask questions such as, "Were you disciplined this way, as a child?" or "Is it hard for you to be a parent now?"

5. Tell them that in order to help them, you must be honest about difficult subjects such as abuse, even if reporting is a result.

6. If abused adolescents seem willing to talk about their abuse and the parents are cooperative in discussing their past, it may be helpful to have the whole family discuss the abuse together for at least part of the session.

7. However, you must intercede if the parents attack their children for making accusations or if they try to influence them (verbally or non-verbally) to stop talking about their abuse. See the children individually then.

8. Seek immediate protection for the children if they seem in danger of future abuse or under pressure to retract accusations. Call protective services.

9. If you have seen the whole family in counseling, but the abuse is disclosed in a session without the offender present:

    • Inform the parents that you must report the abuse before you contact the authorities if their child does not appear to be in danger. This may help to foster a good therapeutic relationship. Tell them what you will say and what your recommendations will be. For example, you may feel that their child does not need protection or the family can learn new parenting skills through continued counseling.

    • To repeat, contact the proper authorities before contacting parents if there is any concern for the child's safety.

    • You may feel that your relationship with the parents will be severely damaged by notifying them of your intentions to report them to child protection services. If so, having the Protective Services Worker meet with you and the family is often helpful. The family then has an

opportunity to discuss their personal issues in a
setting where the therapist can give support and
the Child Protection Service worker can provide
protection for the victim.

INFORMATION PARENTS NEED

When you introduce families to therapy for the first time,
it is important to give them guidelines describing your
therapeutic process. This allows you to take a leadership role.
Since abusive families are often distrustful of outsiders, you
must state your intentions clearly and follow through on your
plans.

Explain that it will be helpful for you to coordinate
services with any other professionals that they are seeing. Let
them know that it may also be helpful for you to talk with
professionals they have seen in the past. Accordingly, ask
their parents to sign forms giving you permission to make
specific contacts. Then, keep them informed of the outcomes.
Try to have the entire family present at most case planning
and coordinating meetings to emphasize how important a role
they play in your treatment plans.

You should also give the family an estimate of how many
groups sessions are recommended and what the duration of
treatment. If the offender is expected to leave the home
make this clear.

And finally, cost and arrangements for payment should be
clearly discussed. No one should have any questions about
times, procedures, expectations or costs that are left
unanswered unless absolutely necessary. Let them also know
the limits of your responsibilities.

Explain the importance of their attendance. Let them know that they must pay for missed appointments no matter how high or low a fee is charged. Such a policy will decrease your level of frustration. It will also reinforce one thing: both parties will know the rules and must suffer the consequences of violation. However, you should not shame anyone for missing an appointment. Set times well in advance for appointments. Decide how flexible a schedule will be allowed outside of regular hours and stick to it. You will then be less likely to feel used by clients who tend to practice manipulation in their dealings with others. Of course, you too must model clear boundaries for your clients. When you reduce your feelings of anger and frustration, you are less likely to shame clients for taking advantage or abusing their privileges.

THE FIRST SESSIONS

It is very important that when you work with families that you establish rapport with each family member. When co-therapists are involved, each therapist may develop a special connection with certain members. It is easier to empathize with clients when therapists appreciate how their individual backgrounds and feelings affect their responses during therapy.

Asking Initial Questions

In the first sessions, talk with the family so that each realizes that he or she has feelings and thoughts apart from the group. In the first session, you will work to:

- Develop rapport

- Let clients express their feelings

- Bring their secrets out into the open

It is often helpful to begin with the family member who is least involved in the abuse. This is often a child whom other family members assume knows nothing about the abuse or is simply not affected by it. The child may ask basic questions about what has happened in the family in a tone that is gentle or sad. When you elicit reactions from this person, the other members may realize that abuse effects the entire family and that they can talk about their secrets. The scenario might unroll like this:

Therapist: "Johnny, do you know why your family is here today?"

Johnny: "I think it's because of incest."

Therapist: "Do you know what incest is Johnny?"

Johnny: "No"

Therapist: "Who would you like to ask?"

Johnny: "Mom"

Therapist: "Mom, do you want to answer that?"

Mom: "Daddy had sex with Susan, Johnny. He was touching her where he shouldn't have. Do you understand?"

Johnny: "Um hum."

Therapist: "Did you know something unusual was going on in your family?"

Johnny: "Well, Susan got all dad's attention and I didn't get any."

Therapist: "Was that sad for you?"

Johnny: "Um hum."

Therapist: "Would you like that to change?"

Johnny: "Yes."

Therapist: "That's something we can work on here."

If they are present, talk with other non-abused children in the family, and then talk to the non-abusive parent. Ask the parent questions that acknowledge that abuse occurred while being supportive. For example:

- How did you find out about the abuse?

- What did you do then?

- How are you doing now?

Next talk with the victim about the abuse and how he or she is feeling now. For example:

Therapist: "How did the abuse come out?"

Susan: "I heard a speaker at school talk about abuse, and started crying. My friend made me go talk with the school social worker."

Therapist: "Then what happened?"

Susan: "Well, they called the county and dad got picked up and now he has to go to court, all because of me."

Therapist: "You took a step to take care of yourself, but you feel bad that you dad has to go to court."

Susan: "Yah. I wouldn't have told if I knew that would happen."

Therapist: "I understand that you feel bad about your
dad going to court, a lot of times kids don't
like some things parents do, but they still
care about them. Perhaps we can help your
family keep the parts you like and change the
parts you don't like."

Notice that the therapist listened to Susan protect her
father without discrediting her point of view.   Instead, the
therapist introduced new ideas ("You took care of yourself")
without forcing them upon the client.

Last of all, talk with the offender, operating on the
assumption that he or she was, indeed, the abuser. Encourage
him or her to talk about feelings but do not allow the offender
to deny or minimize the abuse. A good way to do this is to
ask about his or her reactions to what the others have said:
"How was it listening to your family today?"

Identifying Other Problems

In the initial family assessment, chemical dependency
issues and psychiatric needs should be addressed.   If a
member's chemical use appears to be problematic, arrange for
an assessment since he or she cannot look openly at family and
individual issues until the chemical abuse is addressed.   You
may want to propose a non-alcohol contract for all members.
A thorough psychiatric intake should also be done which
addresses the history of mental illness and current functioning
in the family.   Referrals for psychiatric or physical needs of
clients should be done at this time as well.

ADVANTAGEOUS SETTINGS

Whenever possible, use a therapy setting or combination of settings that best helps you meet the needs of each family. These settings include: peer groups, individual sessions for each member, family sessions, group sessions consisting of more than one family, and marital sessions.

Peer Group Settings

It is often beneficial to involve family members in peer groups before family therapy is initiated. Parents may join women's and men's groups to explore their childhoods and talk about current abuse. We have members present autobiographies as a way of exploring how they became who they are.

Peer groups provide a place for members to identify and discuss issues with others who are struggling with similar problems. Since abusive families are often secretive and isolated, members feel less alone when they meet with others who share their experiences. It helps those who are enmeshed in the family to gain a broader perspective. Group meetings also allow members to let go of the shame they feel. They may find that others accept them even after knowing their most devastating secrets. For members who have been separated from families by emotional or physical abandonment, the group provides a temporary second family. Within the security of a properly functioning group, people will develop as individuals and grow in new relationships.

Many will acknowledge, perhaps for the first time, that they were abused as children or that they saw others abused. If they are to recover from their experiences, they must allow themselves to remember how they felt during that time of their lives.

Self-esteem is intimately bound with personal beliefs about abuse. When members are honest about their feelings and come to understand the myths surrounding abuse (for example, that the victim is somehow responsible), they will be more self-accepting. They will become less dependent upon others and less manipulative. They will be more able to change their old patterns of behavior within the family.

We have also found that acknowledging the pain of their own childhood abuse helps offenders to be more honest about their reasons for abusing others. They see how hiding their feelings as children helped them to survive but that they no longer need that crutch.

The goal is that offenders will accept responsibility for their abusiveness. This is a very difficult task. Offenders are usually more receptive to peers when it comes to talking about abuse. The members will confront those who deny their responsibility for abuse or who refuses to look honestly at their problems.

Spouses of offenders in a peer group setting can explore their own childhoods, their choice of partners, their knowledge or lack of knowledge of abuse, the guilt or shame they feel for not being able to prevent it, and any other actions that kept the family dysfunctional. They can also explore issues such as identification, assertiveness, sexuality, and communication within the family.

Family Sessions

Family sessions, whether they are held with individual families or groups of families, allow members to talk about abuse and related issues and to learn new behaviors. Groups help to decrease the sense of isolation and increase the trust each member feels for others. Other therapy goals include creating new boundaries, strengthening the marital relationship (if the couple stays together), developing parenting skills, decreasing shame, and fostering healthy communication.

5

Responsibilities in Therapy

No therapy session, whether on a one-to-one basis or as a group of three or more, will be successful unless all parties carry out certain responsibilities. In fact, it is the exercise of these responsibilities that determine whether you as a therapist will succeed in reducing or ending the abuse of any victim.

OFFENDING PARENTS

A very important goal for family therapy is to help offenders accept responsibility for their abusiveness. The family must share in this understanding so that the victimization of the child can be permanently ended. You may lay the groundwork for developing healthier relationships between abused children and their abusing parents in both individual and peer group sessions—then do further work in family sessions.

Ask or tell the offending parent:

- Will you tell _____ how you feel about the abuse now?

- Tell _____ how you feel about him or her.

- Tell _____ how you think the abuse affected/will affect him or her.

- Are you sorry about the abuse?

- Tell _____ that you are sorry (if that is the case).

Then allow the victim to express reactions by asking such questions as:

- Why did the offender abused him or her?

- How did the offender's own problems contribute to the abuse?

What is most important is that the offender acknowledge his or her responsibility and show remorse and caring for the victim. It is often helpful for the therapist to point out dynamics as they occur. For example, is the victim thinking more about the offender than him or herself?

The ultimate goal is for adolescent victims to be able to express to their parent offenders their feelings about the abuse. Peer group (see Treatment Strategies) and/or individual sessions help victims prepare for this encounter. They will come to acknowledge the abuse, realize that the parent was responsible, and feel strong enough to talk with their parent about it. Without adequate therapy victims see only rejection, anger, or punishment as possible outcomes, and do not think about their feelings and thoughts and their right to express them.

The following is an excerpt from a therapy session where the offender acknowledges the abuse and the victim expresses her feelings:

Offender: "I want to take time today to talk about the abuse . . . _____, please listen to what I have to say, and then I will listen to whatever you want to say... The abuse was totally my fault. I made you feel like it was your fault so that you wouldn't tell. I tried to stop many times, but I didn't know what to do. I feel terrible about what I've done . . ."

Therapist: "Do you worry about how this has affected her, or how it will affect her in the future?"

Offender: "Yes . . . well, I see you using drugs a lot and I know you don't have many friends right now. I think that if I'd let you go out more, you'd have more friends. I know what it's like to get hurt and what happened to me. I don't want that to happen to you. I care about you, but more like a daughter. Before I used you I thought of how I wanted you. I want to be a better parent and I'm working on it. I want to listen to whatever you have to say to me."

Victim: "I am so mad at what you did to me. I trusted you, and you used me. You made me do things that were gross. I can't imagine ever being able to have a normal relationship with a guy. The time that made me feel the worst was ..."

It is sometimes helpful for the teenage victim to address her parent offender first. Then they are less likely to be overly concerned or protective of their parent in subsequent discussions. This may help them to feel stronger and more in charge.

NON-OFFENDER PARENTS/VICTIMS

Conflicts between the non-offending parent and the victim may be addressed in one or both family sessions and parent-child sessions. If the offending parent and victim were very close and the non-offending parent and victim relationships were distant, jealousy may have developed. Non-abusing parents may see their child as a threat, blame them for causing problems in their marriage, and charge them with causing the abuse.

Non-offending parents, like their children and their offending spouses, need to understand the dynamics of abuse, especially their responsibilities as adults. This message may have to be repeated many times. It helps non-offending parents to assume responsibility for the consequences of their behavior when they and their children tell each other how they felt when the abuse was taking place. You should expect that the children will:

1. express anger that their non-abusing parent did not protect them from their abusive parent;

2. wonder why their non-abusive parent was not respon-
    sive enough to their needs; and

3. feel angry and hurt about what they perceive as their
    non-abusive parents' lack of caring.

On the other hand, non-abusive parents may:

1. wonder why they were not told by their child that he
    or she was being abused;

2. wonder, rightly or wrongly, why their child "flirted"
    with their offending parent; and

3. feel hurt, angry, and jealous about their abused
    child's experiences.

Airing these thoughts and feelings—and knowing that the
other person is listening—often resolves misunderstandings and
allows the family members to feel closer to one another.

If parents and children are of the same sex, it may be
helpful to discuss the sex roles they played in their family and
the changes they are now making. For example, sometimes
mothers will confide that they were abused as children and felt
they had little to offer men as adults. As parents examine
their pasts and learn new patterns, they may be able to offer
empathy and support for their children, as well as new models
to follow.

Both parties may need to make apologies to clear the air.
Non-offending parents may apologize for not picking up clues,
not acting to protect their children sooner, or not being strong
enough to provide better parenting. Children sometimes
apologize for expressing their feelings in abusive ways.

NON-ABUSED SIBLINGS

Non-abused siblings are also likely to feel emotionally neglected. They too need a forum to express how they feel and what they want now from the others in the family. It is very common for siblings to wonder if their abused sister or brother liked being abused. Conversely, the abused child will likely want to know if his or her siblings knew about the abuse.

CONFLICTS BETWEEN PARENTS

Some issues between partners may be discussed in family sessions while others are better suited to couple sessions. Parents of abused children often have a lot of anger and very poor skills for resolving their conflicts. Anger is intensified by the parents' mutual belief that "I can't live with you, and I can't live without you." You need to encourage both parents to question that assumption and replace it with a healthier one: "I am a whole person. I can choose to stay with you and work on a good relationship. I can also leave, and I won't fall apart." They can validate each other by listening to the others' statements and positively reinforcing their strengths. It may be helpful to begin couple therapy by having both partners prepare a list of changes they want and their resentments of the other. These lists should be shared at a couples session.

The next step is for parents to discuss these issues. That may begin by helping them express feelings to each other. You may want to use a "Feeling Wheel" to help them identify emotions in a specific situation. This allows partners to focus on a single event and to admit to or recognize more than one of two feelings. You may prepare a "Feeling Wheel" for their use or have them make one themselves.

Diagram of Feeling Wheel

You may also want to set up a structure for partners to use when they get upset. This structure can help partners break old communication patterns:

Partner 1: I have something to talk with you about. When (explain situation), I felt _____. Please let me know that you heard what I just said.

Partner 2: You said _____, and you felt _____.

Partner 1: Yes. (or) No, you missed _____.

Partner 2: You also said _____.

Partner 1: Right. In the future, if _____ happens, I will _____. I would like you to _____. Are you willing to do that?

Partner 2: Yes. I am willing to _____. (or) You would like me to _____. I am not willing to do that yet. I want to _____ first.

If Partner 2 isn't willing to do what Partner 1 wants, Partner 1 may want to state what the consequences will be.

Partner 1: If you do not _____, I will _____.

Encourage both parents to make statements that begin with "I." By using "I" statements, clients exercise control over their own actions and recognize that they cannot control the actions of others. This makes their partners less defensive.[1]

---

[1]For more information about enhancing communication among partners, see *ALIVE AND AWARE*.

The following are issues that couples may need to explore:

- any current abuse of their children;
- abusive behaviors toward one another;
- whether to stay together;
- their parenting roles and responsibilities;
- social intimacy; and
- sexual intimacy.

Non-abusing spouses may want to know if they were inadequate partners and the other's reasons for abusing their child.   They may get angry at their offending spouse for hurting their child or for hurting and rejecting them.

Partners often need help in opening up channels of trust, affection, and intimacy, and in changing their dependency patterns. To do this, you should reinforce those spouses who are quiet and submissive when they show any initiative.   You should also encourage the parents to make decisions together. Not only does this reinforce the parents' concept of the marriage as a partnership, but it will demonstrate to their children that their parents are a team and have their own separate relationship within the family.[2]

FAMILY COMMUNICATIONS

You should stress the importance for family members to communicate their needs to each other.   Remind them that a lack of openness is what helped to maintain the abuse.   Let

---

[2]For information on couples group therapy for sexual offenders, refer to R. Taylor, 1984.

them know that open channels of communication will help the victims of abuse feel supported by their siblings; thereby, the imbalance of power between sexually abused victims and their brothers and sisters will be equalized.

Victims who were physically abused and made scapegoats for many family problems will also find a healthier role in the family when communication is open. Open communications will help all children in a family to:

- avoid the role of parenting siblings;

- see their parents as taking on their responsibilities;

- learn to take care of themselves as individuals and to share with their families;

- learn to make decisions and learn from the outcomes of these decisions; and

- express their opinions and feelings without fear.

All of the above are possible when the parents are willing to listen to their children express their feelings and ideas. You, as a therapist, should work toward a family situation in which the parents appreciate and care for their children because of who they are and for not what they do.

Those parents who have been abusive will most likely need your help with parenting skills. Among the more important skills you will need to help them with are:

- Non-shaming techniques of control.

- Being consistent.

- Establishing expectations that are reasonable.

- How to handle their personal feelings in non-harmful ways.

Non Shaming Skills

Parents must learn to express their feelings or correct their children's behavior without saying things that shame them.   You should teach parents to recognize the kinds of conflict that ensues from the use of shame.   Then, you can help them to find better ways of expressing themselves. Parents will be more receptive to suggestions when they realize that their old patterns have not been successful.

The Importance of Consistency

Parents need help in setting appropriate goals for disciplining and following through to achieve them. First, talk with the parents about the punishment they think right to impose on their child for misbehavior.   Help them negotiate with each other to reach an agreement.   Next, discuss with them how they can best communicate these ideas to their children. Stress to them that:

- their children need to hear very clearly how the consequences for their misbehavior will be different now;

- their children are likely to push for more lenient punishments or restrictions and that they may even wish that family life was as it used to be when they had more freedom and could do as they pleased;·

- they as parents, must be consistent.   (Sometimes parents feel guilty about the abuse and want to renege on what was agreed to as proper punishment for misbehaving.   This will cause more families problems in the long run. When children do not know what to expect they often feel insecure. They then turn to manipulation and their true feelings are not aired. Parents can stop this pattern by refusing to be manipulated by their children; and

- when parents feel that they must change their minds, it should be based upon sound judgement.

Parents' Expectations

Parents who have been abusive will benefit from understanding childhood development. When they know how children develop in stages, they will be better able to accept their children's behaviors. They will then set expectations for their children that are appropriate for their ages.

Sometimes parents punish adolescents for exercising their independence. They may not like their children's hair styles or make-up. You will probably find it helpful to talk with parents about the importance of adolescents establishing their own identities and making choices when they are not hurting anyone else. Encourage them to listen and talk with their children without demanding that they conform to all of their preferences. This does not mean that parents should hold back on setting limits on inappropriate behaviors or holding expectations for their children.

Handling Personal Feelings

All parents inappropriately take their personal feelings out on their children at one time or another. But abusive adults do it more often and more violently—and acknowledge it less than other parents. As parents become more attuned to their feelings and practice healthier communication habits, they will

be less inclined to take out their feelings on their children.
You can support parents by:

- teaching parents alternatives to misdirected emotion
  (for example, parents can be taught to find ways to
  express their feelings about upsetting incidents
  without hurting others);

- helping them to identify moments when they slip into
  old patterns; and

- pointing out healthy changes that you observe in
  them.

NON-INTACT FAMILY THERAPY

Family members whose abusers are no longer in the home
often seek therapy to work on their problems. A misconception that adolescent victims often share is that they are to
blame because their abusing parents have moved out of their
lives. This misconception must be cleared up. Children, young
and old, have many feelings related to the loss of an offending
parent that they need to express. Also, single parents benefit
from peer group support when they explore their problems
regarding parenting, marriage, and future plans.

When a non-abusing spouse remarries, new problems will
arise. Sometimes children have trouble accepting a stepparent
even if that stepparent is good to them and treats them as a
parent should. The children may feel that by liking their stepparent they are rejecting their natural parent. As therapists,
you need to give children permission to dislike the behavior of
natural parents while still loving them. You must also assure
them that it is alright to develop trust for their stepparents at
their own pace and to set boundaries that they feel
comfortable with. Urge parents who have found new partners
to talk with their children about new expectations. For

example: "Joe (the stepfather) will not hit you when you do something he doesn't like. Instead he will explain the consequences of your behavior for you and for him."

When a divorced, non-abusing parent remarries another abusive person, the family will need to deal with an intensification of the problems previously discussed for families that are intact. Of course, there will now be the added problems with which any reconstituted family must deal.

When parents remarry, children sometimes feel abandoned for a second time: the first parent left and now the remaining parent has attached him or herself to a new spouse. This is particularly a problem for children who have been emotionally or physically neglected. Therapists will need to help members of these families find ways to be close and meet their needs of love and attention in healthy ways.

Frequently, abusive parents who leave marriages never visit their children. This situation deeply affects the children's sense of self-worth and is, therefore, an important one to discuss in therapy sessions.

When children are in foster or adoptive homes, even more problems arise. The parents may believe that, if their children act "normal," go to school or get jobs, everything is fine. They may have trouble accepting the fact that therapy takes time and that their children's feelings may only come out gradually.

Many victims are very difficult to live with. Foster and adoptive parents must realize that, although they cannot change the past, they can help by listening to their children share their thoughts and feelings. They must learn not to take it personally if their children push their limits, set up fights, or act more immature than others their age. The parents should avoid power struggles and remain consistent in parenting.

Therapists should give such parents support and show empathy for the frustration of parenting. Without this help, foster and adoptive families can become abusive. Also, these families might give up their children, resulting in even more feelings of rejection and abandonment among victims of adolescent abuse.

6

Treatment for Adolescents

Professionals are alerted to adolescent abuse in several ways. Some adolescents straightforwardly report their being abused. Others hint at what has happened to them. Sometimes it is their friends who tell. In our agency, we ask all clients, assuming that anyone may have been abused.

However, before you pose any questions about abuse, you should let your clients know what you must report and what you will hold in confidence. In most communities, therapists are required to report suspected child abuse. It is critically important that you explain this to your clients immediately. If you fail to provide this information, they may feel re-victimized, having openly discussed their experiences only to find that they will be reported to the authorities.

One successful way of informing clients who are underage of your obligation to report abuse is to include such information in your description of therapy rules: For example, "I will keep everything we say confidential, except if you are going to hurt yourself or someone else, or if someone has been hurtful to you."

If necessary, describe "hurtful" as sexual or physical abuse. Also let your young clients know that their parents or guardians have legal access to their records. Explain that most parents will let their children have meetings in confidence if you arrange sessions to discuss their progress. The following is one way of approaching adolescents about abuse:

> "I have been concerned about you because of how you have been acting lately." (Be specific). It is my experience that, when people act like this, there is something bothering them. Is something happening at home or somewhere else that is not okay? Is someone being hurtful to you—like being sexual with you when you don't want to be, or hitting you? I care about you, and I want to help."

Our agency has developed an abuse protocol which therapists use at all intake sessions, regardless of any initially apparent problems. This protocol which follows, helps us to determine the nature and extent of any victimization of our clients. If you use this protocol, carefully note any clues of abuse as they fill out the forms and discuss their responses with you.

AN ABUSE PROTOCOL

Read each statement and check if it sounds true for you.

1._____Someone in my family has put me down and made me feel stupid.

2._____I have had scratch marks or bruises after someone in my family hit me.

3._____Someone in my family has hit me with a spoon, a belt, or some other object.

4._____I feel uncomfortable or bad about the way someone in my family touches me.

5._____An adult has touched me or asked to see my sexual parts or has asked me to touch his or her sexual parts.

6._____Someone in my family sometimes gets so angry that he or she breaks things or hits someone.

7._____The police have come to my home because people were fighting.

8._____Someone has forced me to have sex when I did not want to.

9._____Someone in my family has threatened to hurt me or send me away.

10._____Sometimes there is not enough food to eat in the house.

11._____My parents are not around my home very much.

Sometimes you will suspect that an adolescent was or is being abused even though they do not talk about it. If this is true, you may want to talk about how other victims felt when first questioned. Describe how frightened and threatened other people have felt. This often helps to establish rapport and gives them more time to sort out their feelings. If your clients are still unwilling to talk, explain that some offenders threaten that bad things will happen to their children if they tell.

Because victims feel very alone in their problem, it helps them to know that others who have been abused are getting help. Talk to them about how abuse affects people and assure them that no victim needs to face abuse alone. Let young people know that you and others will help. If they still choose not to talk about abuse (perhaps afraid that they will lose the support of their families), tell them that you understand their decision. Tell them that you are available to help them if they later want to talk about it.

TALKING ABOUT ABUSE

Once teenagers acknowledge that they have experienced abuse (whether or not they perceive their experiences as such), talk further about it. Our policy is that in the initial stages of therapy, we should determine all relevant experiences of a client.

We attempt to determine:

1. who the abuser was (Was there more than one perpetrator? Was the perpetrator an acquaintance or a stranger?);

2. the frequency and occurrence of the abuse; and

3. the nature of the abuse.

There are many ways of learning about adolescent abuse. However, do not interrogate victims and you should not expect to get all the details at once. Obtaining much of the information is the responsibility of the police or child protection workers. Some therapists feel it is their responsibility to discover the exact nature of the abuse early in the therapeutic relationship by interrogating victims. This tends to alienate victims. Victims need time to feel safe with their therapists before sharing their painful experiences.

Some victims, however, want to tell their therapists everything in their first session. Unfortunately, many of them may then feel shame and will not return to therapy. As a cautionary step, you may want to urge your clients to check out and make sure that they trust you before divulging sensitive information.

It is also important to use language appropriate to your client's age and maturity. Many victims do not know words such as ejaculation, penetration, or fellatio. Find out which words they use and define for them the words that others use. This information will be useful to them, especially if they have to talk about their abuse to authorities.

To repeat, abused adolescents, as well as adults, often answer questions and talk about their abuse without perceiving their experience as abusive. They may believe rationalizations given by their offenders that:

- they deserved what happened;

- their parents were only showing affection;

- what was done was alright because it was done by their parent; and

- that their was nothing done that was wrong. (Such as "we didn't have intercourse, so it's okay.")

As a therapist, you should carefully challenge such beliefs by describing ways in which abusive experiences are harmful. Throughout the therapy process, you should help your young clients to rethink these issues.

Some of your clients may acknowledge their abuse but be unwilling to give even a general description of what their experience has been. Our policy has been to respect that need and postpone questioning until a more solid therapeutic relationship has been established. It is essential to remember that many victims feel very distrustful and will retreat if they feel pushed to disclose information that is too threatening or painful to them.

Adolescent victims are more likely to talk openly about their being abused when they realize that:

- they have, without success, repeatedly tried to stop the abuse;

- someone in their family must try and stop the abuse;

- they are becoming abusive toward others and may abuse their own children in the future; and

- that their progress through adolescence has been disrupted.

When you talk with adolescents about how important it is that abuse be reported, they often have many questions. They will be concerned about how their families will react. The ones who have abused them will probably have told them that terrible consequences will ensue, such as going to jail, their parents will get divorced, others will not believe them, they will be physically punished, or even that they will be killed. In addition, they may have been taught that people outside of their family cannot be trusted. Adolescents are likely to believe that some of these possibilities are likely to occur if they report their parents.

In addition, adolescents are often concerned about their younger siblings. They may wonder who will take care of them if they leave home? (Frequently teenage victims are caretakers in the family.) They may also be concerned that their brothers or sisters will become victims if they leave. Many abused adolescents are willing to tolerate being abused in order to spare their siblings.

All of these are problems that adolescents, their families and their therapists need to discuss. You should remind your clients of their need for help, in taking care of themselves. Reassure them that you and others will do everything possible to protect them and get them additional help. Point out that they can become models for their brothers, sisters and even a non-abusing parent by refusing to accept abuse.

Of course, all abused adolescents are vulnerable to threats from home. Therapists must, therefore, provide the support and encouragement they need.

REPORTING ABUSE

If you must report something to protective services, it is a good idea to have your client on another phone line when you make the initial call. This makes the procedure less mysterious and allows your clients to be active participants. Then, make arrangements for the worker to visit the therapist and client, together, before contacting the family. This will give your client an opportunity to establish rapport and share more information. Next, plan to meet with adolescent and family along with the child protective services personnel, if so approved by the case worker in charge.

After being notified by authorities that someone in their family has reported abuse, families are often shocked and defensive. If some do not believe that abuse has occurred, which is often the case, your clients may be the recipients of anger and rejection. It is helpful to engage numbers into therapy at this point if it is not already in progress. If families refuse therapy, there are ways to encourage them. If all efforts through the court system fail, at least you should assist your clients in making their own life choices.

Most abused adolescents, whether their families choose to come for counseling or not, need support from their families after the secret has been exposed. If rejected by their families, adolescents will need even more support from you and other adults in their lives. You may want to increase therapy in order to minimize anxiety, solidify the therapeutic relationship, and reinforce the view that they do not deserve abuse but they do deserve to get help. Encourage contact with people they can trust and turn to for support—other adults and friends, as well as other victims they meet in peer group sessions.

Abused adolescents usually need advocacy services as well as supportive counseling. It may be advisable to inform protective services of your concerns, especially if you feel that your clients are in unsafe or unsupportive environments. If cases are not opened formally by protective services because of lack of information, it may still be helpful to continue supplying them with information you learn.

Once abused teenagers or others report on their abuse, certain outcomes are likely. Your abused teenage clients are likely to:

- feel relief that their secret is out in the open and that the abuse may stop;

- still feel a strong allegiance toward their families;

- wish that they had denied that abuse occurred;

- feel guilty for having placed family members in the hands of the court, even if they are angry at them; and

- feel anger and caring for the same people, at the same time.

All of these feelings can be very confusing for adolescents. It will help if they are able to acknowledge to you both their regrets and their relief. It is not usually beneficial for adolescents to deny the positive aspects of family life or their need for their families.

INDIVIDUAL THERAPY

It is generally most effective to begin therapy on an individual basis. That way, the relationship between therapist and client can develop in a private setting. The client can begin to trust at least one person and sense that coming to therapy is worthwhile. Many clients begin therapy with low self-esteem and few positive relationships. Individual therapy can be a situation where clients receive positive, caring attention, as well as supportive guidance. When relationships become stronger, therapists can effectively confront clients in caring ways. Without such a relationship, clients may regard confrontation as shaming and believe they are being told that they are a bad person.

Individual therapy should be a prelude to group therapy for some clients. It does not always work to begin peer group counseling without a certain amount of personal strength, often achieved through individual therapy. Without it, some clients feel afraid and leave the group.

For others, individual therapy needs to be continued to supplement group therapy. Some victims are in extreme need and will require more than once a week group sessions. Others need individual therapy to prepare them to discuss difficult subjects in family or group sessions. Clients involved in both individual and group therapy should not be permitted to discuss subjects necessary for group discussion in their individual sessions, unless it is to prepare for talking in their group.

GROUP THERAPY

Group therapy is an extremely important mode of treatment for sexually abused adolescents. Victims should be placed in groups with six to eight peers of the same age level and sex. In some groups, we have both a male and female leader. In others, we have two leaders of the same sex as the group members. There are advantages to both combinations of group leadership. Same gender leaders with the same gender clients sometimes offer more cohesiveness: women can collectively recognize their strength; men can be vulnerable as well as tough. However, mixed gender groups offer flexibility. For example, clients may open up to the leader of the sex with whom they feel most comfortable. Also, sexual myths can be dispelled, such as women being passive and men being mean with mixed gender groups.

Before a client joins a peer group, each member should be seen for an intake session. Look for those signs that group therapy is appropriate: clients should be able to verbalize reasons for wanting to join a group, they must be able to act assertively enough to speak up in the group and not be psychotic.

Intake is also a time to clarify group rules and the program (to follow). The rules and steps should be introduced in the first group session that clients attend. Every client should be asked to make at least an eleven-week commitment to the group before joining; this is very important since victims are sometimes irresponsible and live a chaotic crisis-to-crisis lifestyle. If they lack family support, their commitment to the group is even more important.

"Open-Ended" Groups

Your clients should begin group therapy when they are ready and as soon as there are openings. They should also terminate their membership when it is clear that it is hurting the group or they can no longer benefit from the experience. Some members will have recently joined, others will be "old hands." The members will be working on different problems at any one time. This provides new members with models to follow.

The group should meet for two hours weekly, with quarterly, day-long workshops. The weekly sessions should have a basic structure, although they may vary depending on the clients particular needs.

Typically, the session should begin with a brief "check-in." All of the members should describe how they feel and share something about the previous week. Next, the members should negotiate for time. They ask for time to discuss their concerns. The group should then decide who needs time and how much.

Halfway through a session, the group should take a five to ten minute break. The break is important because it enables the group to become more cohesive and it helps the members to improve their socialization skills.

Ten minutes before the end of the group, the members should evaluate the session and make a closing statement (often the Serenity Prayer.) Then, they should each write in their notebooks about how the group went for them, how they feel about their progress, and what their next accomplishment will be.

Members of each group should make up most of the group's rules and change them as needed. Some groups make rules about how to ask and negotiate for time, and whether and when to have breaks and special groups. Confidentiality is a basic rule for all members—with the exception of the leaders. The leaders must be able to report the possibilities of suicide, harming others and abuse.

A "Five Step" Program

Completing a "five step" program is the minimum requirement to graduate from a group in our agency. The "five step program" helps a client deal with certain problems in as short a time as eleven weeks. However, therapy for some victims must continue for as long as a year or more. Our "step program" allows for such differences in attendance.

The steps provide a structure within which abused adolescents discuss difficult problems safely, yet assertively. The program is presented to new members at their first session. With this outline, they receive notebooks for keeping assignments and keeping track of their progress. Each of the steps come with exercises that members complete as homework. When they have finished an assignment, they share it with the group.

Also when new clients join the group, old members explain their reasons for being in the group and share something about themselves by way of introduction. New members are also asked to explain why they want to join the group. Sometimes the group chooses to talk informally for a short time in order to get to know each other better. Old and new members ask questions about school, music, and so forth. Then, the old members explain how the group operates and they let the new members know that their input is welcomed and desired.

Step 1.   The "Five Step Program" begins for the members with their writing autobiographies, in as much detail as they choose. They then share them with their groups. This gives all members an opportunity to get to know one another better and to discover the experiences they have in common. In the process, they usually examine their own lives more closely and gain more understanding of themselves. We encourage them to identify ways in which their experiences have affected their personalities and behaviors.

Step 2.   Next, the members assess their strengths. Then, they look at aspects of their personality and behavior that they think need changing. Identifying personal strengths is often difficult for clients whose sclf-esteem is low. If they have trouble, they are usually asked what they like about themselves. Tell them that it doesn't matter how trivial it seems. You may suggest that they ask the other members, their friends, or their family about their possible positive qualities.

Creating a list of those characteristics in need of change is usually not difficult for teenagers who have been abused. However, it may be risky for clients to admit before the group that they are vulnerable and need to make changes in their lives. This is true, especially when they have had to show toughness or indifference to survive at home. You will need to encourage your clients to do as much as they are able. However, do not force them to reveal more than they choose.

The second part of Step 2 involves goal-setting. Goal-setting is particularly important for victims who find themselves in destructive situations, but have no tools for making changes. This occurs when victims learn early in life that they have little power and that no one listens to them or considers their needs.

Step 3.   The third and probably most important step is for the client to talk about the abuse that occurred. Victims need to talk about what they think has happened, express their feelings, examine their beliefs, and look at how abuse has affected them. They should be asked to complete the exercise as it pertains to every type of abuse they have experienced and repeat it as often as necessary.

Then each victim is asked to write a letter to their offender expressing their feelings about being abused. The letter is a valve for expressing feelings that, if unstated, develop into depression and feeling ashamed. Such letters help victims to understand that it was their offenders who were responsible for their being abused.

Having written such a letter, many clients choose to do further work. Some are willing to role play a discussion with their offender or with other people who in their abusive environment (the non-offending parent, for example). We encourage those clients who are also in therapy with their families to share this information during those sessions. For clients whose families are not in family therapy, the clients should schedule sessions to talk with their offenders when their counselors can be present.

Step 4.   The fourth step looks at how clients have hurt others. Therapists need to make it clear that everyone in the group, at one time or another, has hurt another person. Some clients may say that they have physically abused siblings or have had sexual experiences with a family member that has hurt that person, too. Some may realize that they have used sarcasm or provoked verbal arguments to take their anger out on others.

As part of this process, you must help the group members to take responsibility for their actions. Explain that they need not feel ashamed for what they have done but that they can, and indeed should, learn how not to harm others.

Then, the members should be asked what they can do to make amends to people they have wronged and how they will behave differently in the future. You should provide structure, support, and encouragement to help them work to achieve their goals.

Step 5.   The fifth, or "good-bye" step is goal assessment. The members assess their progress while in the group. They describe what they were like when they first joined, what they worked on, and how they see themselves as they are ready to leave the group. Those who remain in the group may contract to repeat one or more of the steps or work on new personal goals that are appropriate to pursue in a group setting. Those who are terminating their participation should discuss their plans and goals.

After each person speaks, group members and leaders provide feedback and say good-bye. The feedback gives members and leaders a chance to praise the person leaving and to note areas that person may choose to work on in the future.

OTHER NEEDS

Many victims blame themselves for their abuse. Thus, they may need to hear over and over, sometimes for months, that they are not to blame. Therapists need to repeat this message patiently, making sure it is heard and understood by listening to their clients express their feelings and ideas.

Clients also need to give constructive feedback to the other members. Clients who refuse to believe that they are not to blame for their own abuse sometimes convince other members that they are blameless for being similarly abused. By helping others, these clients soon learn to excuse themselves.

Self-Esteem Enhancement

Many victims feel low self-esteem, because they were raised in families where they were regularly belittled. That they are also victims of abuse is yet another scarring source of shame. Sharing their "secrets" with peers and supportive adults in the group will help to erase some of these scars. When they see that the group does not reject them, but rather likes them, their self-esteem improves. They begin to believe that they are likeable because the group likes them. The successes they have in following the "Five Step Program" is also self-affirming. Step 2, in particular, enables victims to explore their positive qualities and to recognize that change is possible.

Developing Trust

Adolescent victims of abuse are accustomed to being manipulated and mistreated. The very people that they should have been most able to trust have abused that trust. As a result, they may initially miss appointments in order to test your commitment and concern. You can support clients by recognizing this need to test limits by clearly communicating your expectations. These expectations should be applied consistently. Any failure of your clients in meeting your expectations should not be dealt with by shaming them. If clients behave inappropriately during group therapy and sus-pension becomes necessary, tell them clearly what they need to do to resume therapy.

You also help them identify their feelings and allow them to develop trust in you and the others at their own pace. It may be helpful to work with clients having serious trust issues in individual therapy before introducing them to group therapy.

Healthy Intimacy Needs

Similar to lacking in assertiveness skills, many abused adolescents do not understand what is necessary in having a healthy intimacy with others. Victims are often frightened of getting too close to people. Female victims often talk about how they have no close girlfriends; and worse for some, their only relationships with males are sexual in nature. Male victims often find it difficult to express their feelings or to touch either girls or boys. Group therapy should offer clients an opportunity to trust and enjoy their peers. Friendships can and should develop as the members realize that they share experiences and that they care about one another. You can initiate discussions about closeness and touching that enable the group to discuss the kinds of intimacy that are healthy.

Sexuality is a highly charged topic for all adolescents and for victims of abuse, in particular.

- Adolescents who have been sexually abused by someone of the same sex, an experience very common for male victims, may wonder if they are homosexual. It is very important that you let your clients know that they can make choices about sexuality and that being abused by someone of the same sex does not make one gay or lesbian. Help them to explore their options if they seem willing and interested.

- There will be some sexually abused adolescents who become sexually active with members of the opposite sex; thereby, seeking to prove to themselves that they are not homosexual. These clients need to talk about their abuse and their sexual preference as well as their use of others to satisfy their own needs.

● Some sexually abused young people become sexually overactive because that is the only way they know how to relate to others. They may believe that sex is all that they can offer another person. For their attitudes to change, such clients must develop greater self-esteem. Feedback from leaders and other members of the group about their relationships may help them to gain a better perspective.

We occasionally use various other exercises, especially during day-long workshops, to deal with sexuality and sex roles. One example of this is when we have members make a collage about women's or men's roles (expectations and possibilities) and then have them explain why they chose certain pictures. You may also use worksheets that ask them questions about body image, what they like about themselves, and what they wish was different. There are many excellent activity books available for use with therapy groups, several of which are included in Appendix B.

Using films and speakers is also effective for dealing with sexuality. We have shown films on acquaintance rape, incest, and sex roles. We have also brought in guest speakers to discuss sexuality. Adolescent victims often know very little about the human reproductive system, contraceptives and pregnancy. Sometimes, those who do know and are sexually active do not use birth control responsibly. By discussing sexuality openly, therapists can disseminate important information and give adolescents a chance to learn.

When Victims Act Like Victims

Many teenage victims approach life with a helpless, passive demeanor. They are vulnerable to being manipulated by others. When their therapists follow a therapeutic process that helps them to increase their self-esteem and be more assertive, they will behave much less like victims and be less likely of being victimized. Adolescents who need special coaching may want to roleplay situations in which they must stand up for themselves. Group members can often help them to look critically at that behavior which puts them in vulnerable positions.

Understanding One's Proper Role

Abused adolescents particularly need to explore their roles in the family. They can do so—apart from their families—in group therapy by completing the Five Step Program and working on their personal problems. This will help them to gain new perspectives on themselves, their problems, and make better choices. At the same time, they may influence a better relationship with their parents and siblings. Family sessions can be a natural outgrowth of peer group or individual sessions. For sexually abused adolescents whose families choose not to participate, peer group therapy can function as a source of strength and support. It will help them deal with feelings of loss, fear, and anger.

Grief

Many sexually abused adolescent victims experience grief. They may have lost parents as a result of neglect,

abandonment, divorce, or death.   They may be alienated
because they have been raped, molested, used, and deprived of
their right to personal boundaries.   Yet, they often grieve the
loss of those who have abused them.   However, your clients
need to grieve these losses and rebuild their strengths.
Resources for relieving grief are also included in Appendix B.

7

Needed Adjunctive Services

Many sexually abused teenagers will show abuse-related symptoms such as chemical dependency, food disorders, physical problems, and suicidal tendencies. In such cases, it may be critically important that the services of other professionals be coordinated with your abuse therapy.

SUBSTANCE ABUSE

When substance abuse is discovered, there are four steps that should be taken:

1. Consult with or have a preliminary assessment done by a chemical health specialist. Adolescents may be asked to keep a log of the illicit chemicals they use, their feelings before and after use, and the effects of their use.

2. These teenagers may then be asked to decrease their use of alcoholic or other drugs and use alternate ways of dealing with their feelings. It may be recommended that they attend an alcohol therapy program.

3. If these adolescents are able to decrease their use of mind altering drugs, a non-use contract may be prescribed.

4. If they are unable to comply, the recommendation should be a thorough chemical dependency assessment and follow through with whatever treatment for substance use is indicated. Until adolescents stop using chemicals to avoid facing their problems, treatment for abuse will be ineffective.

FOOD DISORDERS

Many victims of sexual abuse suffer from anorexia, bulimia, or compulsive overeating. When these disorders are discovered, it is important to assess the severity of the disease.

1. If clients are in physical danger, confidentiality must be broken so that parents can be notified and treatment for their food disorder begun. In most cases, there is time to help clients make the choice to seek help.

2. If clients suffering from food disorders deny that they have problems and they resist referral to an eating disorders program, the following questions may help them examine their problems.

    • Do you eat food to dull painful feelings?

    • Do you pride yourself in controlling your hunger?

- Do you eat so little that you are unable to function effectively?

- Do you exercise excessively?

- Is food used as a treat in your family?

- Is food taken away as punishment?

- Have people told you that they are concerned about your weight?

As abused teenagers who are also suffering from eating disorders look more and more at the realities of their use of food, their defenses gradually decrease. Since eating disorders are common among abuse victims, there are usually other group members who can confront and support them in examining food abuse.

3. When your clients who are suffering from eating disorders are ready, refer them to therapists or programs specializing in eating disorders. If they can be seen on an outpatient basis, you should coordinate therapy for abuse with the eating disorders therapist.

4. If your clients do not choose to seek help on their own, making it a requirement for continued therapy may be necessary. Hiding behind food is similar to hiding behind chemical abuse: the issues are covered up and progress is severely limited. Further information on eating disorders is included in Appendix B.

PHYSICAL PROBLEMS

When adolescents complain of physical problems, you should recommend that they see a physician. Some sexually abused victims will be reluctant to seek medical help because they are ashamed of their bodies or they do not believe others care. They may be particularly frightened of pelvic examinations. Encourage your clients to get help by offering them your support and concrete recommendations. You may suggest that they bring along a friend, read a pamphlet explaining their disorder, or talk more about it with someone they trust. Remind them that they deserve to have a healthy body and that they are worth caring for.

SUICIDE

When a teenage client shows even the slightest sign of being suicidal, a suicide assessment should be done. If the danger of suicide is present, notify your client's parents or guardians. If you need assistance in assessing suicidal potential or treatment, there are mental health professionals available in most communities who have special training and experience in the area of suicide. They should be contacted.

Case Coordination

You may need to have contact with many professionals and lay persons in your community. It is important to coordinate case plans with therapists working with other family members, county social workers and lawyers involved with the adolescent. You may also need to refer your clients to agencies that deal with pregnancy, childbirth, adolescent parenting, abortion, prostitution, mental health or job seeking. In referring them, it is important that all services a client receives be coordinated. You may be the one who must do this coordination. Working for your young clients with other agencies and individuals may be required of you, especially if no other adult is looking out for them.

8

After Termination

The length of time a sexually abused teenager is involved in treatment varies according to his or her particular needs and circumstances. Eleven weeks is the minimum we allow for group participation. It is difficult to accomplish much in less than three months. The average length of treatment is about one year. (Some will be ready to handle life without further therapy.) When your clients feel ready to terminate, some will still need continued assistance in other programs or groups. Termination is a time to acknowledge the growth that has taken place and to identify issues needing further work, either on their own or in therapy.

As they grow older, they will encounter new challenges and new situations that will spark memories of their sexual abuse and old behaviors. For many, involvement in a significant relationship will bring issues to the surface that may not have been dealt with in your therapy sessions. For example, they may find it hard to maintain a positive relationship with a boyfriend or girlfriend.

These and other problems may bring your clients back to you or to other therapists. It is important that you communicate this long-term perspective when your clients are terminated. It will help them to accept their imperfections and reinforce their strengths. It will also increase the likelihood that they will seek further therapy if needed before they regress too far.

It will also help if you contact your clients in three months and, again, one year after discharge. Your calls may serve as catalysts for their seeking further help if they are in such need. Most will be very pleased that you have contacted them and flattered that you care about how they are doing. Some will resume therapy at this point.

These young clients who have survived abuse and opened up to others in therapy about their experiences are often strong and likeable people. Most have learned new and healthy ways to care for themselves and others. The abuse is no longer a secret tearing them apart. This base of self esteem and new skills will aid them in tackling future life problems. Most will seek therapy or open up to family or friends when they need help. They have done an excellent job—and you have helped. Thanks for caring about kids.

APPENDIX A

The Five Step Program

Session	Agenda
1	Introduction of group members and the structure of group therapy sessions.
2-3	STEP 1. Share your autobiography with the group.
4-5	STEP 2. Share your list of strengths and needs; set at least one goal.
6-7	STEP 3. Talk to the group about how you have been abused and how you feel about it.
8	STEP 3. Share your letter(s) with the abuser and any other people you choose to write to.
9-10	STEP 4. Talk to the group about how you have been hurtful to others and how you feel about it.
11	STEP 5. Tell the group how you feel about the progress you have made in group and in your life generally, and where you want to go from here.

ADOLESCENT GROUP STEPS

STEP 1

Who am I?

This step helps you to get to know yourself better. You will think about what your life has been like up to now and how all these experiences have affected you.

Directions:

Write an autobiography and share it with the group.

GUIDE FOR AUTOBIOGRAPHY

An autobiography is your story about your own life. Read through the questions below. You may want to include some answers to these questions as you write your autobiography.

About Your Family

Where were you born?
What is your place in your family? (oldest son, second oldest, etc.)
How did you get your name?
What is the first thing you remember? What is the feeling connected with that memory?
Who were the people in your life?
What were they like? Who was the most special to you?
Who cared the most about you?
How did your mother/father treat you?
How did family members show affection?

What kind of person did your mother/father think you should be?
What kind of kid were you?
What was your favorite thing to do?
What did your family do for fun?
What made you happy?
What made you sad?
What is the best thing that has happened in your family?
What is the worst thing that has happened in your family?
How do you feel about yourself?

About Grade School

Where did you go to grade school?
How did you feel in school?
What did you like/dislike about school?
What were your favorite subjects?
What were your worst subjects?
At recess, where did you play?
Who did you play with? What did you do?
How would your teachers have described you?
How would your classmates have described you?
What were your successes?
What were your failures?

Did you or any of your family have any health problems?

Describe any changes in your family—moving, deaths, divorces, etc.

How did your parents get along?

Adolescence

What was school like for you?
Good parts?

Bad parts?
How would your teachers have described you?
How would your classmates have described you?
What were your successes?
What were your failures?
How did you spend your free time?
Did you or any of your family have any health problems?

Describe any changes in your family patterns: moving, deaths, divorces, etc.
How did your parents get along?
Settle differences?
Handle stress?
What was your family's religious practice?

About Yourself

What is your biggest accomplishment?
What is your biggest failure?
What is the best thing your family has done?

About the Future

What kind of person would you like to be as an adult?
Make three wishes for yourself.

ADOLESCENT GROUP STEPS

STEP 2

Part A

What do I like about myself, and what do I want to change about myself?

Part A helps you to name your strengths and needs.

Directions:

Make a list of your strengths (what you like about yourself) and your needs (what you want to change about yourself).

Part B

I believe I can take more responsibility for what I do and how I feel.

> If you're not sure where you're going,
> you will not know how to get there
> and may not even recognize it when you do.
>
> a Greek fable

Part B helps you to set goals

To feel better about yourself, you have to be willing to change, to try new ways of doing things. Goals are targets you want to aim at. You reach goals by changing how you behave. When you set a goal, you must answer three questions.

- What do you want to change?
- How do you plan to change it?
- How can you tell whether or not you succeed?

Directions:

1. Pick one or two things you would like to change about yourself or your life, or things you want to feel better about. (Refer to your list of needs in Part A).

2. Set your goals for change. Be sure to write down you plans for all three questions about goals in your notebook.

3. Share your goals with the group.

4. Report to the group on progress toward your goals, and ask for feedback.

Repeat STEP 2 as many times as you want to.

ADOLESCENT GROUP STEPS

STEP 3

I have been abused.

This step will help you to write and talk about how you have been abused and how the abuse has affected you. By abuse, we mean that someone has neglected you or hurt you physically, sexually, and/or emotionally.

You may have many strong feelings as you do this step. So ask for support from people you can trust, such as group members and counselors. Remember, you are not alone. Many other people have been abused, too, and had feelings like yours.

Part A

1. Write down how you were abused and who abused you.

   • How were you abused? Physically? Sexually? Emotionally? Through neglect?

   • In what ways were you hurt? (For example: Were you hit with a belt buckle? Did you have intercourse?)

   • How often were you abused? (Every day? Every week?)

   • How long did the abuse last? (Six months? Two years?)

2. Write down a description of one time when you were abused. Share it with the group.

- What happened?

- Who else was around at the time? How did they react?

- Were you threatened or tricked into thinking that the abuse was okay?

- Were you told to keep the abuse a secret?

- Were you threatened that something bad would happen if you told someone?

3. Write down how you felt about the abuse.

- How did you feel at the moment the abuse was happening?

- How did you feel afterwards? (about yourself? about the abuser? about other people for example, the other parent, men or women)?

- Did you have feelings about the abuse happening again? What were they?

- Have you blamed yourself for bringing on the abuse? Why? What did you feel you did to cause it?

- What do you think about blaming yourself——if that's what you did? (What you feel and what you think can be different.)

4. How did the abuse affect your life when it was happening?

- Did you worry about the abuse happening again?

- Did you think about the abuse?

- Did you lose sleep? Have nightmares? Have a hard time concentrating in school? Begin using (or use more) alcohol and drugs? Lose friends? Spend a lot of time thinking about how to avoid abuse (such as staying away from home)?

- Did you get in trouble with the law?

- Did you become more sexual than you wanted to or than was good for you?

- Were you depressed, suicidal, or hurtful to yourself in other ways?

- Were you aggressive (for example, get into fights)?

5. Were there parts of your relationship with the abuser that were somehow positive for you?

- How did this relationship meet some of your needs?

- How do you feel about having these needs met in this way?

- Would you rather have had your needs met in other ways? If so, how?

6. How has abuse affected your life now?

- How do you feel about yourself?

- How do you relate to other people?

- What parts of question 4 are still problems for you?

Part B

Write a letter to the person (or people) who hurt you. Tell them what they did to you and how you felt (or still feel) about it. You will not have to send this letter. Then, share the letter with the group. If you want to, do a role play in the group, talking with the person who hurt you. You may also want to talk with the abuser(s) in counseling sessions about the things you wrote or talked about.

Write letters, if you like, to other people—such as family members, too.

ADOLESCENT VICTIM STEPS

STEP 4

I admit that I have done things that were hurtful to other people.

This step will help you to take responsibility for ways that you have been hurtful to others without blaming them or making excuses.

Sometimes, when you have been hurt by others, you react later by hurting people yourself. This can happen because you cannot take your anger out on the person who hurt you. So, you take it out on someone who is weaker than you are. Or sometimes, you abuse someone else because you have learned that it is a way you get some good things, such as a temporary feeling of closeness and love, or a relief from tension. If either of these situations apply to you, you may have had a role in hurting someone else. This does not make you a bad person. So, don't put yourself down. You can change the way you act with other people.

Directions:

1. Write down ways that you have been hurtful to others. Answer these questions for each person you may have hurt.

    ● What happened, exactly? If this happened many times, give some examples.

    ● How were you feeling about yourself before you were hurtful? About the other person?

    ● How did you decide who you would treat in hurtful ways?

- Did you think (or hope) that what you did would meet some needs for you? Which needs?

- How did you feel about yourself afterwards? About the other person?

- Did you want to stop acting this way? If so, did you try to stop? Did it work?

- How do you feel now about the things you did?

2. Write down ways that you will make it up to the people you hurt.

- What do you want to say or do?

- When are you going to do it?

- Who do you want to be there?

- How can you avoid doing these hurtful things in the future?

- How can you make sure that your needs are met in healthy ways?

- What can you do every day to make sure you replace unhealthy patterns with healthy ones?

3. Make sure that you set goals for changing hurtful patterns if you didn't already do that in STEP 2, Part B. Follow the same procedure as in STEP 2, Part B.

ADOLESCENT VICTIM STEPS

STEP 5

This step helps you to say goodbye to the group.

When you and your counselors feel you are ready to leave the group, prepare a graduation talk. In it, share ideas and feelings about how you have changed. Be sure you answer these questions in your talk:

1. What were you like when you first started group?

2. What changes have you made?

3. What do you like or dislike about group?

4. What things about yourself or your life would you still like to work on?

Then, get feedback from the group about how members have seen you change.

If you will be continuing in group, answer these questions:

1. What steps will you contract to do again, in more detail?

2. What other goals do you want to work on?

APPENDIX B

Bibliography

Statistics

1. Minnesota. Social Services Division, Community Services Department. Hennepin County Child Protection: *Selected Statistics.* 1970-1984. Minneapolis.

2. Colorado. American Humane Association: *Highlights of Official Child Neglect and Abuse Reporting.* Denver, 1983.

3. Colorado. American Humane Association: *Highlights of Official Child Neglect and Abuse Reporting.* Denver, 1981.

Abuse

4. Finkelhor, D. "The Sexual Abuse of Boys." *Victimology: An International Journal,* 1981, 6 (1-4), 76-84.

5. Giareto, H. "Humanistic Treatment of Father-Daughter Incest." In: R.E. Helfer and C.H. Kemp (eds.), *Child Abuse and Neglect."* Ballenger Publications, 1976.

6. Gutheil, T.G. and Avery, N.C. "Multiple Overt Incest as Family Defense Against Loss." *Family Process,* 1977, 105-116.

7. Nakashima, I., and Zakus, G. "Incestuous Families." *Pediatric Annals,* 1979, 8 (5), 29-42.

8. Sarles, R.M. "Incest: Symposium on Behavioral Pediatrics." *Pediatric Clinics of North America,* 1975, 22, (3), 633-642.

9. Brandt, R.S.T. and Tisza, V.B. "The Sexually Misused Child." *American Journal of Orthopsychiatry,* 1977, 47 (1).

10. Gibbens, T.C.N.; Soothill, K.L. and Way, C.K. "Sibling and Parent-Child Incest Offenders." *British Journal of Criminology,* 1978, 18 (1), 40-52.

11. MacMurray, D. "The Effect and Nature of Alcohol Abuse in Cases of Child Neglect." *Victimology: An International Journal,* 1979, 4 (1), 29-45.

12. Anderson, D. "Shame proneness versus guilt proneness in incest victim as opposed to non-incest victim groups." Unpublished master's thesis. University of Minnesota, Minneapolis, MN. 1979.

13. Kaufman, I., Peck, A. and Taguirer, C. "The American Constellation and Overt Incestuous Relations Between a Father and Daughter." *American Journal of Orthopsychiatry,* 1954, 24, 255-279.

14. Browning, D.H. and Boatman, B. "Incest: Children at Risk." *The American Journal of Psychiatry,* 1977 (January), 134 (1): 69-72.

15. Anderson, L.S. "Notes on the Linkage Between the Sexually Abused Child and the Suicidal Adolescent." *Journal of Adolescence,* 1981 (June), 4 (2), 157-62.

16. James, B., and Nasjlet, M. *Treating Sexually Abused Children and Their Families.* Palo Alto, California: Consulting Psychologist Press, 1983.

17. Miller, J.; Moeller, D.; Kaufman, A.; Divasto, P.; Pathak, D. and Christy, J.   "Recidivism Among Sex Assault Victims." *American Journal of Psychiatry.* 1978, 135 (9).

Abuse and Delinquency

18. Alfaro, J.D.   Report on the relationship between child abuse and neglect, and later socially deviant behavior.   In: R. Hunner and Y.E. Walker (eds.) *Exploring the Relationship Between Child Abuse and Delinquency.*   Monclair, New Jersey: Allanhedld, Osman and Company Publishers, Inc. 1981.

19. Gruber, K.J. and Jones R.J.   "Does Sexual Abuse Lead to Delinquent Behavior?   A Critical Look at the Evidence. *Victimology: An International Journal,* 1981, 6 (1-4), 85-91.

20. Smith, C.P.; Berkman, D.J. and Frase, W.M.   Reports of the National Juvenile Justice Assessment Centers.   A Preliminary National Assessment of Child Abuse and Neglect and the Juvenile Justice System: The Shadows of Distress. American Justice Institute, 1979.

Runaways

21. Lukianowicz. "Incest I, Paternal Incest."   *British Journal of Psychiatry,* 1972, 120, 301.

22. Armstrong, C.   "660 Runaway Boys."   Boston: B. Humphries, 1932.   Cited in "Runaways in History," Lipshutz, M.R. *Crime and Delinquency,* July 1977, 329.

23. Carper, J. "Emergencies in Adolescents: Runaways and Father-Daughter Incest." *Pediatric Clinics in North America,* 1979, 26, 883-894.

24. Howell, M.C.; Emmons, E.B.; Frank, D.A. "Reminiscences of Runaway Adolescents." *American Journal of Orthopsychiatry,* 1979, 43, 883-894.

25. Lourie, I.S.; Campiglia, P.; James, L.R. and Dewitt, J. "Adolescent Abuse and Neglect: the Role of Runaway Youth Programs." *Children Today,* 1979, 27-30.

26. Robey, Ames; Snell., J.E.; Rosenwell, R. and Lee, R. "The Runaway Girl: a Reaction to Family Stress." *American Journal of Orthopsychiatry,* 1963, 33, 310-311.

27. von Houten, T. and Golembrewski. Adolescent Life Stress as a Predicator of Alcohol Abuse and/or Runaway Behavior. Washington, D.C.: National Youth Work Alliance, 1978.

Prostitution

28. James, Jennifer and Megliding, Jane. "Early Sexual Experience as a Factor in Prostitution." *Archives of Sexual Behavior.* 1978 (January), 7 (1), 31-42.

Family Therapy

29. Bowen, M. *Family Therapy in Clinical Practice,* 1978, New York: Jason Aronson.

30. Satir, V. *Conjoint Family Therapy,* 1964. Palo Alto: Science and Behavior Books, Inc.

31. Minuchin, S.   *Families and Family Therapy,* 1974, Cambridge: Harvard University Press.

32. Anderson, L. *Personality and Demographic Characteristics of Parents and Incest Victims.* 1977. Unpublished manuscript. St. Paul, Minnesota.

33. Lustig, C.P.; Dresser, J.W.; Spellman, S.W. and Murray, T.B.   "Incest: A Family Group Survival Pattern." *Archives of General Psychiatry,* 1966, 14:31-40.

Communication

34. Miller, S., Nunnally, E. and Wackman, D.   *Alive and Aware: Improving Communication in Relationships,* Minneapolis: Interpersonal Communications Programs, Inc.

35. Taylor, R.   "Marital therapy in the treatment of incest." *Social Case Work,* 1984 (April).

Parenting

36. Dinkmeyer, D. and McKay G.   *The Parent's Guide Systematic Training for Effective Parenting of Teens, Circle Pines,* Minnesota: American Guidance Service, 1983.

37. Dreikers, R.   *Children: The Challenge,* New York: Hawthorn/ Dutton, 1964.

38. Buntman, P., Saris, E. *How to Live With Your Teenager: A Survivor's Handbook for Parents,* New York: Ballantine Books, 1979.

39. Clarke, J. *Self-Esteem: A Family Affair,* Minneapolis: Winston Press, Inc. 1978.

40. Alberti, R.E. and Emmons, M.L. *Your Perfect Right.* San Luis Obispo, California: IMPACT. 1974.

41. Lazarus, A.A. *Behavior Therapy and Beyond,* New York: McGraw-Hill Book Company, 1971.

42. Smith, M. *When I Say No, I Feel Guilty. How to Cope Using the Skills of Systematic Assertive Therapy,* New York: The Dial Press, 1975.

Sexuality

43. Blaink, J. *The Playbook for Kids About Sex.* Burlingame, CA, Down There Press, 1980.

44. _____. *The Playbook for Men About Sex.* Burlingame, CA, Down There Press, 1981.

45. _____. *The Playbook for Women About Sex.* Burlingame, CA, Down There Press, 1982.

46. Comfort, A. and Comfort, J., *The Facts of Love.* New York: Ballantine Books, 1980.

47. Ingleman-Sundberg, A., *A Child is Born: The Drama of Life Before Birth.* New York: Dell Publishing Company, Inc., 1974.

48. Johnson, E., Love and Sex in Plain Language, New York: Harper and Row Publishers, Inc., 1965.

49. Mooney, T., Cole, T. and Chilgren, R. *Sexual Options for Paraplegics and Quadriplegics.* Boston: Little Brown and Company, 1975.

50. Man's Body: An Owner's Manual, The Diagram Group, 1977. New York: Bantam Books, Inc.

51. Mayle, P. *What's Happening to Me?* New Jersey: Lyle Street, Inc. 1975.

52. Scanzoni, L. and Mollenkott, V. Ramey. *Is the Homosexual My Neighbor? Another Christian View. San Francisco: Harper and Row Publishers, 1978.*

53. *Sisley, E. and Harris, B. The Joy of Lesbian Sex.* New York: Simon and Schuster, 1977.

54. Woman's Body: An Owner's Manual, The Diagram Group, New York: Bantam Books, Inc., 1977.

55. McCoy, K. and Wibbelsman, C. *The Teenage Baby Book.* New York: Simon and Schuster, 1978.

56. Pomeroy, W. *Girls and Sex.* 1981, New York: Dell Publishing Company, Inc.

57. _____*Boys and Sex.* 1981, New York: Dell Publishing Company, Inc.